I0810929

PLANTS AGAINST THE PATRIARCHY

Written by JP Hawthorne, 2017
Illustrated by Iris Misciagna
Originally published in 2017
This edition © Microcosm Publishing, 2023
ISBN 9781621066583
This is Microcosm #645

For a catalog, write or visit:
Microcosm Publishing
2752 N Williams Ave.
Portland, OR 97227
www.Microcosm.Pub

To join the ranks of high-class stores that feature Microcosm titles, talk to your rep: In the U.S. Como (Atlantic), Fujii (Midwest), Book Travelers West (Pacific), Turnaround in Europe, Manda/UTP in Canada, New South in Australia, and GPG in Asia, India, Africa, and South America. Sold to the gift market by Faire and Emerald

If you bought this on Amazon, we're so sorry because you could have gotten it cheaper and supported a small, independent publisher at Microcosm.Pub

Global labor conditions are bad, and our roots in industrial Cleveland in the 70s and 80s made us appreciate the need to treat workers right. Therefore, our books are MADE IN THE USA.

ABOUT THE PUBLISHER

Microcosm Publishing is Portland's most diversified publishing house and distributor, with a focus on the colorful, authentic, and empowering. Our books and zines have put your power in your hands since 1996, equipping readers to make positive changes in their lives and in the world around them. Microcosm emphasizes skill-building, showing hidden histories, and fostering creativity through challenging conventional publishing wisdom with books and bookettes about DIY skills, food, bicycling, gender, self-care, and social justice. What was once a distro and record label started by Joe Biel in a drafty bedroom was determined to be *Publishers Weekly*'s fastest-growing publisher of 2022 and #3 in 2023, and is now among the oldest independent publishing houses in Portland, OR, and Cleveland, OH. We are a politically moderate, centrist publisher in a world that has inched to the right for the past 80 years.

Global labor conditions are bad, and our roots in industrial Cleveland in the '70s and '80s made us appreciate the need to treat workers right. Therefore, our books are MADE IN THE USA.

BROOM *Cytisus scoparius* *Ally of the Sun*

In the age of instant relay-and-replay, it can be hard for some to keep from falling into the deep well of despair when peering into current events on the world stage. And for some, this deep well of despair can be addicting—thinking "what's next?! What could be worse than *this*?!" At times, we might catch ourselves, mindlessly and even obsessively checking social media, news outlets, podcasts, political commentary, or reading the horrific comment section of articles.

Broom is an essence for those who are constantly confronted with the ugliness and evilness of the world and feel victimized by the news and the world around them. Depressed about the future of this planet and their lives, falling into pessimism, hopelessness, and inaction. Broom does two things to address this:

1. Gives an optimism, a flicker of hope, showing us in which way we can use our anger, despair and depression in hopes for a better future. Seizing world challenges as learning opportunities for growth and change. The plan will look different for everyone, but some examples might include:

    - Getting educated on topics close to your heart, then talking with friends, family about the issues.
    - Volunteering for organizations that align with your values.
    - Participating in group discussions, town halls and community forums outside your comfort zone.
    - Putting boundaries on news and information consumption to keep from overwhelm and falling into despair.

And because we are getting educated, getting involved and learning more about how to strategically be of service to the world, with Broom, we gain a greater consciousness around how we choose to approach life. More attention is paid to our daily thoughts and actions, with the intention to respect ourselves and others. A conscious choice to represent self with greater integrity, virtue, and strength through servant leadership.

2. Magically speaking, Broom helps us by representing ourselves or living in a more virtuous way, showing the world by example what we *do* want. We participate in creating a group intention, a kind of group-mind, we add to the mass consciousness or collective vision for what we want. Some call this a 'thought-form'. We are shifting and changing the world into a place we want to live in. Of course this does not substitute direct and indirect political action, but it is one magical approach to a more just world.

"Never forget that justice is what love looks like in public." —Dr. Cornel West

CALIFORNIA POPPY

Eschscholzia californica — *Ally of the Sun*

Indicated for those who seek to find a light outside of themselves to attach. The type could be obsessed with media-culture, sports players, Hollywood celebrities, the glamour of party life or drug use. Or even with certain spiritual practices. Seeking to collect spiritual experiences that only serve to build the ego, distorting the spiritual identity without doing the inner-work that's required. Some may call this 'spiritual materialism', and can sometimes lead to bordering on cultural appropriation.

Seeking light outside, without taking proper time to engage our shadow selves, we never learn to grow or enrich our lived experiences on the catalytic playground we can earth, which facilitates our evolution as conscious beings. California Poppy helps to break illusions and expose false forms of "light". Redirecting the need for spiritual connection to be *centered in self*, rather than outside oneself, reducing the need for validation or approval from others. If we expand this to the dominant culture, this maybe a remedy for those who declare "love and light". Unwilling to look at the ugly shadow of our nations historical and present atrocities. Unable to look at the terrifying conditioning and programing we all have hiding in the recesses. Disgusted by the thought that they may harbor notions of racism, bigotry, xenophobia, misogyny, transphobia, etc.. Sidestepping responsibility, asserting exemption as a person who is "full of light".

"Your vision will become clear only when you can look into your own heart. Who looks outside, dreams, who looks inside, awakens." — Carl Jung

OREGON GRAPE

Mahonia aquifolium or Berberis aquifolium — *Ally of the Sun*

Oregon Grape grounds in the solar plexus and increases trust in one's own gut, creating more reliance in the self to make the right decision and take the right action when a challenge is presented. It raises self-esteem and more importantly self-worth, recognizing original patterns of why these issues are on board in first place. These patterns can begin as early as childhood, especially if one had experienced a form of poverty, whether mild, extreme, or temporary. Where resources were scarce or non-existent. Oregon Grape helps to get clarity with our feelings around money, financial security, values, social mobility, and internalized classism. It might also help those who have conflicting feelings about capitalism, wanting to make money for their own financial stability but also have a strong desire to stay true to one's working class background, or personal values within anti-capitalistic frameworks.

"The first lesson of economics is scarcity: there is never enough of anything to fully satisfy all those who want it. The first lesson of politics is to disregard the first lesson of economics.
—Thomas Sowell

Are You Afraid of the Dark ?
2017

ST. JOAN'S WORT *Hypericum perforatum* *Ally of the Sun*

St. Joan's Wort is thought to help people to cope with standing in the light and fully being seen. For working through shadow material, seeing oneself as a whole being. Exposing the fragmented, shameful, discarded and hidden parts. Encourages acceptance to those less-than-lovable shadow pieces we tend to hide from others and push away from ourselves. Benefiting from St. Joan's Wort are those who may have a fear of the dark or the unknown, fear of being exposed, resistance to vulnerability, or exhibit paranoia. The flower essence may also be indicated for those who are having a hard time due to past-life experiences related to being exposed.

St. Joan's Wort is magically important to protection workings. Especially those involving psychic attack or negative thought-forms. Or sudden unexplained fears before stepping out and being public. St. Joan's Wort protection is similar to being out in the Sun itself. Often people feel safe or protected during the day, this is a similar feeling SJW grants. (Of course, this is not to suggest that the night is be to feared or degraded. The night or dark, has been vilified in our dominant culture for hundreds of years. Similarly to the protection of the day, the night offers us a different kind of sanctuary.)

SUNFLOWER *Helianthus annuus* *Ally of the Sun*

In its vibrational remedy, Sunflower has the reputation for going deeper into father issues. But what's bigger example of 'father' issues? Sunflower is also about repairing damage done by the out-of-control *global* father. The universal patriarchal system we all live and participate in – those *other* father-issues. With Sunflower, we examine systems and structures of power. Those who have, those who have not. We also look at our own power and relationship to power: the power to disagree, change, dismantle. The power of sustainable solutions for positive change to benefit the masses, including the benefit to non-humans. Sunflower gives us courage to face a heavily patriarchal world through sympathy. By working *within* the system and sometimes *with* the system to understand how it needs to changed. How to best cut the head off of the monster, from inside the monster. Finally, Sunflower equips us with useful strategies to address global "father issues".

Sunflower might be helpful for those who work for an organization or cause antipathetical to their values, like the environmental activist who is a data clerk at Exxon Mobile. Or someone who is pursuing a degree to understand how the system works to ultimately accomplish radical transformation within that field or system, like the witch who goes to seminary school.

Let's Trojan Horse This Shit!

LEMON BALM *Melissa officinalis* *Ally of the Moon*

Engage in the emotional landscape, without losing self in bog. Lemon Balm calms the spirit, renews and refreshes the day, aids in slowing down when worked up. While it may be helpful for sleep, I find it to be helpful taken during the day, especially prior to anxious events like public speaking, or a job interview. Works to balance emotional expressions to give perspective. This plant pops a buffer between our emotions and obligations, helpful for those with a tendency for care-taking, or doing emotionally labor for others, often without compensation and often without recognition. Lemon Balm gives pause, just enough for one to ask themselves "Is this my business?"

VANILLA *Vanilla planifolia* *Ally of the Moon*

Vanilla flower essence is for a general dullness to life or when one is spending too much time at work or at school. Vanilla encourages us to retreat, repose, when we need to withdraw and recuperate. It gives us a sense of security and comfort. Puts us in touch with the needs of our animal body and what some may call "the inner child", opening to caring for oneself in whatever way our heart's desire leads us into for the moment. Releases the worry or need to care for others.

"Caring for myself is not self-indulgence, it is self-preservation, and that is an act of political warfare." —Audre Lorde

Radical Self-Care

WOOD BETONY

Betonica officinalis or *Stachys officinalis* *Ally of Mercury*

Wood Betony crumbles disillusionment, allowing one to see what is the truth at the core of an idea or action. Authors of antiquity mention that Wood Betony might be helpful in dispelling 'ghosts of the head', hauntings of past trauma, reoccurring episodes, or obsessive thoughts which grind and gnaw at an individual. Wood Betony may also be helpful with thought-forms: speaking or thinking something which often is seen realized a short time later either in the body or externalized outside of one's self. Or, it's useful for those who have a strong mind-body connection, whereas physical symptoms manifest as a result of thinking or obsessing over related outcomes. Wood Betony increases the kinship between brain and stomach, or gut. Wood Betony is great for proof-oriented types: those who have damaged the bridge between gut-based instinct and intellectual-knowing. It repairs this connection where intuition meets knowledge.

~~"Control your body if you want your mind to work properly."~~

—Rene DeCates

facts + faith

YARROW *Achillea millefolium* *Ally of Mercury*

Energetically, Yarrow works with boundaries, those who are susceptible to other's energetic influences. Yarrow is useful in distinguishing where one person ends—and another begins. Preventing from any energetic slime from others. Yarrow acts as an astringent, shoring up the fortress to one's energy field. Molding and morphing one's aura to appropriately fit situations and environments. Allowing for malleable ease and grace to navigate—minimizing nasty and jarring disruptions to one's field. Of course, one still receives emotional information, but now with a guarded boundary. Granting authority for what comes-in or-out of one's field and ultimately their body. Yarrow is also helpful in travel magic and frontline support.

APPLE *Malus pumila* — *Ally of Venus*

While this essence improves giving and receiving from the heart and working with imbalanced fear or anger, it also gives a soft assistance around issues related to the body. To fully be present in the body, which can be truly challenging for some in a capitalistic culture that easily praises intellect at the expense of being divorced from our bodies. Considered to be helpful in motivating one to take better care of themselves: improving daily habits like getting more sleep, or remembering to take breaks. This remedy is softly grounding, sweetly patient, and quietly calming.

"To say that I am perfectly content with my body and all the parts that assemble it is nothing less than radical."
—Virgie Tovar

Rage the Pach!

"Yesterday I was clever, so I wanted to change the world. Today I am wise, so I am changing myself." —Rumi

HIBISCUS *Hibiscus rosa-sinensis*

Ally of Venus

According to the Flower Essence Society, Hibiscus is indicated for harm caused from the commercialized abuse of femme sexuality. Helps to restore and reclaim sexuality, creating more accurate and positive models of one's own femme sexuality. Assists in the divorce from unobtainable standards perpetuated in mainstream media, including the notion that Euro-centric beauty ideals are the gold standard. Hibiscus thaws what is frozen inside. It opens one to warmth, passion and living more fully in the body, combining the fire element with the earth element. Hibiscus may encourage dance as an outlet of expression of one's sexuality.

"There is no way to repress pleasure and expect liberation, satisfaction, or joy." —Adrienne Marie Brown

BURDOCK *Arctium spp.*

Ally of Venus

Burdock used as a plant ally, is helpful in addressing patterns of suppressed or misdirected anger, clearing toxicities in the emotional body. Burdock is indicated for those who exhibit traits of toxic masculinity, or patterns of self-depreciation based on internalized misogyny, homophobia, racism, classism, xenophobia, ageism, etc. Burdock helps to loosen patterns and cycles of internalized or externalized anger, hate, despair, bitterness and gives a feeling of working toward a more balance state.

"Listening is a very active awareness of the coming together of at least two lives. Listening … is certainly a prerequisite of love. One of the most essential ways of saying 'I love you' is being a receptive listener."

—Fred Rogers

White 'splain | Man 'splain
Het 'splain | c i s 'splain

LINDEN *Tilia spp.* *Ally of Venus*

The flower engenders sociability. Imagine sitting beneath a tree having a cordial, open conversation. Linden helps us to see that we are all human underneath the façades we carry. We all have beating hearts, high hopes and a need to feel safe and loved. However, we all have very different experiences of life. Linden opens us to the philosophies and ideals of other's *lived* experience without judgement, need to be defensive or to play 'devil's advocate'. The heart and communication softens, engaging in compassionate listening. It may be helpful for the more privileged in relationship to those less privileged. White people who work with people of color for instance. Linden assists with opening the heart and shutting the mouth, leaving room for others to safely voice their experiences. One might consider having iced Linden tea with a parent who has a hard time accepting your sexual orientation or gender expression. Or offer a Linden candy to your neighbor who doesn't share your spiritual or religious framework. Lastly, Linden may be helpful for those with a tendency to man'splain, white'splain, het'splain or cis'plain.

DEVIL'S CLUB *Oplopanax horridus* *Ally of Mars*

Projection is a psychological theory which suggests that humans unconsciously shift their unpleasant reactions, thoughts, and behaviors unto others. Releasing themselves of any undesired responsibility—a type of blame shifting. Devil's Club helps to show us what-is and is-not ours. It helps to block other's false projections from being internalized. Devil's Club is useful for those who are hyper-vigilant based on past abuse, exhaustively looking out for future abuses. Devil's Club may especially be helpful for those who identify in minority communities because transgressions are committed as frequently as everyday, and in small and subconscious forms known as micro-aggressions. Saying "you're pretty for a (*insert race/ethnicity*) girl" is an example of a common and harmful micro-aggression. The perpetrator's belief that Euro-centric beauty is the highest standard is a projection about who-is and who-is not considered attractive in our culture. Again, Devil's Club helps to protect us from internalizing these abuses.

Ethical Consideration

This herb is indigenous to the Pacific Northwest and therefore is not part of the historical European herbal canon. While we should always first ask plants if they will work with us, Devil's Club needs extra attention and sensitivity. Devil's Club has made an agreement with the author of this zine to be included here, but this does not grant blanket permission for use to anyone who reads about it. Please be respectful. Other alternatives would be Elderflower, Oregano, Yarrow, St. Joan's Wort.

Not today Satan !

ELDERFLOWER *Sambucus nigra* *Ally of Mars*

Elder has a long historical significance with witches. I suppose because both witches and Elder hold a connection between the earth realm and death—working with shadow and transformation. Elder helps us to lean into mystery, into the unknown. I recommend the flower essence for those who work in 'death', such as veterinarians, hospice care-takers, or those who have the magical job of being a death doula.

Both now and in the past, witches were considered rebels of society. Those who refused to buy into bogus religious limitations, or patriarchal or social expectations, values, or demands. Elder gives us the courage to say "no" consistently, never swayed. Igniting one's ability as a shit-kicker, boosting assertiveness especially when interacting with bullies, narcissists, gas-lighters, and tyrants. Eliminating and removing the old, wasteful and out-dated. Sparking circulation of vital energy and new blood. Aiding in renewal, regeneration, and rejuvenation.

"Anger is a sign that something needs to change."
—Mark Epstein

Rebel Witch Support

ONION *Allium cepa*   *Ally of Mars*

From how I see it, Onion flower essence works in three ways. The first is to give one the feeling of peeling away old emotional layers, removing what isn't working, toxicity still being carried. Removing layers of grief and sadness and getting to the heart of matters. Like peeling an onion, we shed tears. This process isn't pleasurable and can be vulnerable. Onion breaks open the lie that we are isolated, alone, that nothing we do matters in the slightest. It gives us the awareness that like Systems Theory, one piece, one action, one belief affects the whole in ways both seen *and* unseen.

In the second phase of working with Onion, we learn about how to more appropriately deal with affairs of the world, showing us how we can personally be of support and build strength in ourselves and our community. A need for bonding or belonging to a group larger than oneself while increasing global awareness. Cultivates tolerance and active listening. There's a detached yet fierce compassion with Onion that allows one to care and be involved, but without the incomprehensible pain of the entire world washing into one's heart.

The third phase of working with Onion is similar to the first. While staying informed, aware and engaged with the world, Onion continues to peel off layers of apathy, complacency, despair, and disassociation that are trying to newly form around the heart. Onion is a flower essence we might choose to work with for a month or longer, until one feels that they have achieved the first two phases. Then take Onion for shorter periods of time in order to keep peeling at the heart of all matters as described in the third phase. When we remove layers of what we are not, we get to the core truths of who we really are. This is authentic activation.

"We never know how our small activities will affect others through the invisible fabric of our connectedness. In this exquisitely connected world, it's never a question of 'critical mass'. It's always about critical connections.

—Grace Lee Boggs

CEANOTHUS *Ceanothus spp.* *Ally of Jupiter*

Similarly to Onion, this flower essence exposes the big lie about patriarchy and capitalism—that we are all separate, fending for ourselves to accumulate as many resources as possible. Ceanothus helps us to shatter this complex falsehood by reminding us who we are, where we've come from and what our core truth is. Truth is the headlight to our automobile of life. And capitalism often forces our truth to ride in the trunk, telling us the only way to get ahead is to play along. To compromise and stifle ourselves. Ceanothus shows us our own self-deceptions and what about ourselves we may have buried. When we begin to say no to systems, actions, language, traditions, behavior that oppresses us—when we remove our distractions and refuse to participate in a system that is killing us, then we make room for living purposefully. Living as whom we were created to be—giving birth to hope and healing, birth to what is possible, birth to Divine inspiration.

Don't be surprised if one begins to work with Ceanothus and suddenly quits a job that is making them ill. Or, one discovers unusual and creative ways to get their resources met. This is very important: when working with Ceanothus, be open to possibilities you might not have *ever* considered in the past.

"Possibility is not a luxury. It is as crucial as bread." —Judith Butler

OAK *Quercus spp.* *Ally of Saturn*

Our culture prizes a highly functional, highly productive work ethic, creating a society of over-taxed "worker robots". Our workload can be so great, we don't have a moment to question this unsustainable insanity. Not only does Oak help to restore us from the mental, emotional and physical exhaustion of overwork, it also pulls us out of the product-oriented conveyor belt to see the bigger picture, gain perspective, and examine exactly how much work is actually in the hopper.

Oak won't necessarily make one quit their job, but if one is prone to pile on responsibility, Oak asks "is this the hill you want to die on?" This may forcing one to voice-up the chain of command regarding their reasonable human needs and expectations. Oak types don't like to ask for help, but Oak does teach exactly how to do this in a way that still holds integrity and one's reputation intact.

Lastly, Oak says that we can't do *everything*. It reminds us that we are humans and not worker robots. That we have limitations: mental, emotional and bodily needs. Oak teaches to acknowledge the physical warning signs when we have exhausted ourselves, granting the much needed courage to say "no".

"Love is a combination
of care, commitment,
knowledge,
responsibility, respect
and trust."
—bell hooks

More from www.Microcosm.Pub

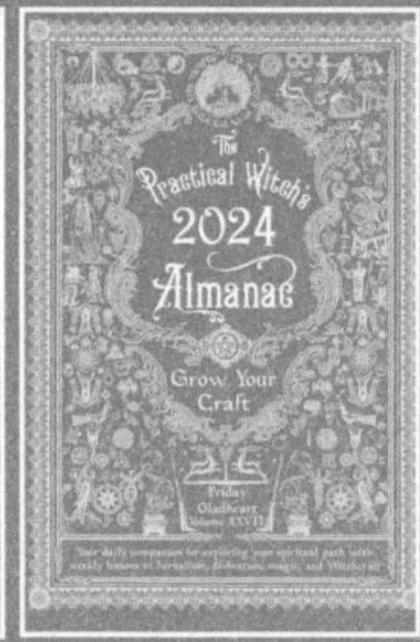

SUBSCRIBE!

For as little as $13/month, you can support a small, independent publisher and get every book that we publish—delivered to your doorstep!

www.Microcosm.Pub/BFF

More books about making it through alive and intact

about the author

JP Hawthorne is a Portland-based queer astrologer, witchy-herbalist and founder of the Portland School of Astrology, the largest astrology school in the U.S.. He began studying astrology in 1995 and has went to school for Japanese language, public health, herbalism and is magically-trained. His work with Cosmophilia includes the marriage of astrology with herbal tradition, hand-making a line of Astrological Herbals including teas, tinctures, essences and sprays. He is currently writing a book on astral-herbalism, as well as a number of zines on the topic. JP's work has been featured at School of Art Institute of Chicago, Portland Art Museum, Portland State University, Nike, as well as various local shops, FM radio shows, conferences, and websites.

JP is available for astrological consultations at www.Cosmophilia.com or for learning more about astrology, visit www.PDXAstro.org.

about the illustrator

Iris Misciagna is an artist living in Portland Oregon. Her love of flowers, and their complex natures, was born in the hours she spent wandering the forests of her childhood home and which now weave through all of her designs and paintings.

©2017 Cosmophilia